Lerner SPORTS

SPORTS ALL-ST★RS

TRAE YOUNG

Elliott Smith

Lerner Publications ◆ Minneapolis

Lerner Publications Company
An imprint of Lerner Publishing Group, Inc.
241 First Avenue North
Minneapolis, MN 55401 USA

For reading levels and more information, look up this title at www.lernerbooks.com.

Main body text set in Albany Std. Typeface provided by Agfa.

Photo Editor: Brianna Kaiser
Lerner team: Sue Marquis

Library of Congress Cataloging-in-Publication Data

Names: Smith, Elliott, 1976- author.
Title: Trae Young / Elliott Smith.
Description: Minneapolis : Lerner Publications, 2021 | Series: Sports all-stars (Lerner sports) | Includes bibliographical references and index. | Audience: Ages: 7–11 | Audience: Grades: 4–6 | Summary: "Atlanta Hawks point guard Trae Young is an up-and-coming basketball prodigy with elite offensive skills. Sports fans will love this high-action book about one of basketball's newest stars"— Provided by publisher.
Identifiers: LCCN 2020023434 (print) | LCCN 2020023435 (ebook) | ISBN 9781728404356 (library binding) | ISBN 9781728423159 (paperback) | ISBN 9781728418810 (ebook)
Subjects: LCSH: Young, Trae, 1998—-Juvenile literature. | Basketball players—United States—Biography—Juvenile literature. | African American basketball players—Biography—Juvenile literature.
Classification: LCC GV884.Y38 S65 2021 (print) | LCC GV884.Y38 (ebook) | DDC 796.323092 [B]—dc23

LC record available at https://lccn.loc.gov/2020023434
LC ebook record available at https://lccn.loc.gov/2020023435

Manufactured in the United States of America
1-48493-49007-9/24/2020

TABLE OF CONTENTS

The Atlanta Hawks and Miami Heat were facing off for the second time of the 2019–2020 season. As he took the court, Trae Young wanted to make up for a mistake.

Trae Young pushes past Goran Dragic of the Miami Heat at their February 20, 2020, game.

FACTS
AT A GLANCE

- **Date of Birth:** September 19, 1998

- **Position:** point guard

- **League:** National Basketball Association (NBA)

- **Professional Highlights:** won a gold medal as a member of the United States U18 basketball team; led college basketball in points and assists during his freshman season at Oklahoma; was the no. 5 pick in the 2018 NBA Draft by the Dallas Mavericks; named an NBA All-Star in 2020

- **Personal Highlights:** won the January 2020 NBA Cares Community Assist Award; started the Trae Young Foundation and the Trae Young Basketball Academy; signed a shoe deal with Adidas

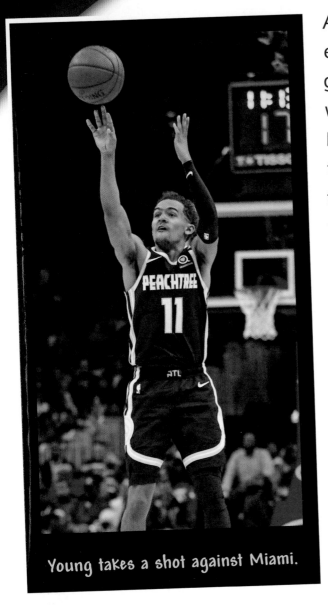

Young takes a shot against Miami.

A couple of months earlier, the Hawks' point guard thought his team was going to beat Miami. He even yelled during the fourth quarter that the game was over. But the Heat came back and won the game. Young wanted another chance to help his team win.

Right away, Young took control. He made long three-point shots. He drove to the basket for layups. And he sank his free throws.

The Heat defenders could barely keep up with Young's drives and long jump shots. But the game was still close. The Hawks were losing by seven points after three quarters. In the fourth, Young took over.

Young pulled up way behind the three-point line and nailed the shot to tie the game. And he didn't stop there. He scored 20 points in the final quarter, pushing his team to a 129–124 win. He finished with 50 points and eight three-pointers, both career highs.

"I was ready to play this game," Young said after the victory. "I wanted to come out and put on a show and try to win. And that was what I did. And it was a great night."

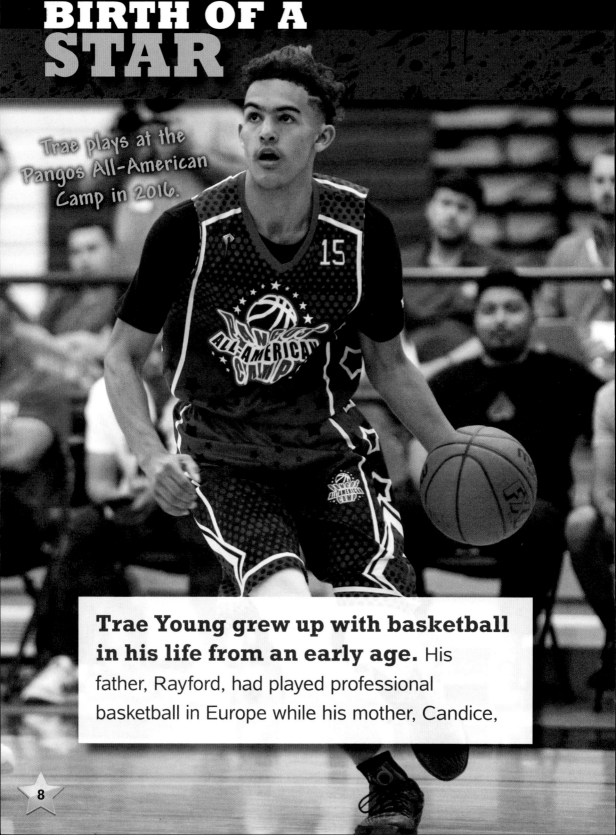

BIRTH OF A STAR

Trae Young grew up with basketball in his life from an early age. His father, Rayford, had played professional basketball in Europe while his mother, Candice,

Young practices with his younger brother, Timothy.

looked after Trae and his three younger siblings. Trae
grew up in Norman, Oklahoma, on a steady diet of drills
and exercises that his father taught him. Trae went to the
local gym at six in the morning before school every day
to practice.

Trae started playing varsity basketball as a high school
sophomore. He was going up against much bigger
players, but he was used to that. Trae had been part of
several elite traveling teams that played tough opponents.

As a kid, Trae helped the University of Oklahoma basketball team by retrieving rebounds during practice. He got players food, water, and towels and did other chores.

Each season in high school, Trae grew stronger and taller. His stats also continued to improve. In his junior season, he averaged 34.2 points and 4.6 assists. By then, several big colleges knew about Trae. He also received a boost after playing for Team USA in the under-18 World Championships in Chile. Trae helped the US team win the gold medal.

Trae had a big decision to make before his senior season in high school. He had gone from an unknown player to a top college prospect. Some of his offers were from Kentucky, Kansas, and Texas Tech, the school where his father had played. Trae decided to stay home. He chose the University of Oklahoma, to the delight of his family. After making his decision, he averaged 42.6 points during his senior year of high school.

At Oklahoma, Young quickly became a standout. In the fifth game of the season, he scored 43 points in a win over Oregon. A few games later, Young tied a college record with 22 assists. He was on his way to becoming one of the top picks in the NBA draft.

Young tries to score for the Oklahoma Sooners in a 2017 game.

Young spent just one season with the Sooners before joining the NBA.

Young was first in the country in both scoring (27.4 points) and assists (8.8) per game. His impressive stats helped the Sooners qualify for the college tournament. After Oklahoma lost to Rhode Island, Young decided he would leave the Sooners and go pro. "I've been preparing most of my life to join the NBA, and that time has come for me," he said.

HARD WORK

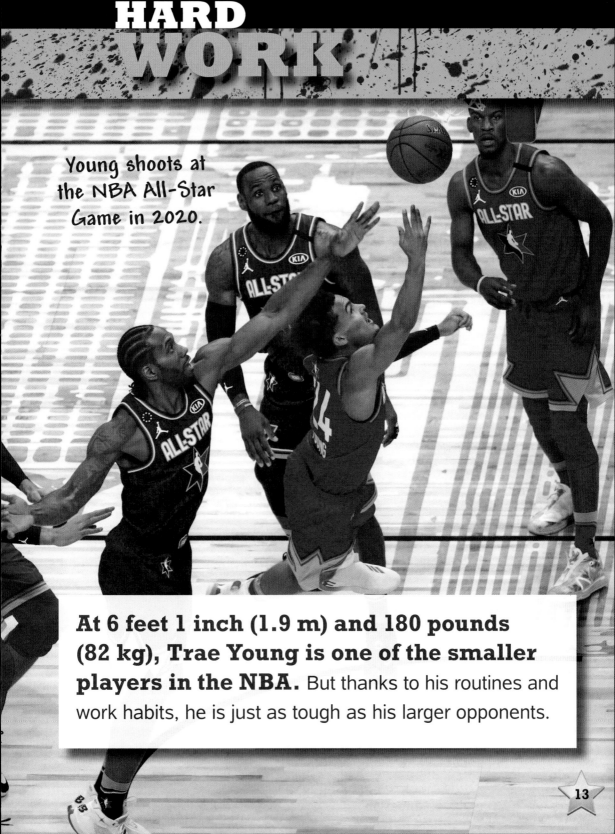

Young shoots at the NBA All-Star Game in 2020.

At 6 feet 1 inch (1.9 m) and 180 pounds (82 kg), Trae Young is one of the smaller players in the NBA. But thanks to his routines and work habits, he is just as tough as his larger opponents.

Young practices a variety of moves and dribbles daily. His behind-the-scenes work results in flashy highlights during games. One of his childhood heroes was point guard Steve Nash. Nash, a smaller player like Young, was known for his passing ability. Young has followed in Nash's footsteps. He continues to watch videos of Nash. The work has paid off. Some experts say Young is the best passer in the NBA.

Through simple head nods, Young can communicate with his teammates on the court. He then delivers pinpoint bounce passes or perfect lobs that lead to baskets.

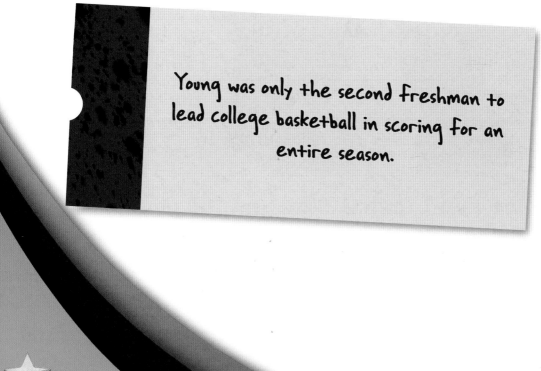

Young was only the second freshman to lead college basketball in scoring for an entire season.

Young readies a shot during a Hawks team practice.

Long-range shooting is another skill Young works hard to perfect. He can launch a shot from anywhere on the court. Fans often compare Young to another great shooter, Stephen Curry of the Golden State Warriors. Like Curry, Young warms up with a lot of three-pointers during practice—sometimes as many as 500!

But Young's secret weapon is his floater, a high-flying shot between a jump shot and a layup. It helps him score when playing against bigger defenders. Young's father had him practice floaters at an early age. He would hold a broom up in the air to act like outstretched arms and have Young shoot over it.

Young shoots a floater in a game against the Los Angeles Clippers.

"It's very important to have that in my arsenal," Young said. "It keeps the defenders who are guarding me off their balance because they do not necessarily know if I'm going to shoot a floater or throw a lob or continue to try to get a layup."

Defense is one area where Young wants to improve. He is usually smaller than the person he is guarding. To help balance the odds, Young exercises to gain weight and muscle. One summer he gained 15 pounds (6.8 kg) of muscle to help give him an edge. Experience in the league also will help Young become a better defender.

Young with (*from left*) Donovan Mitchell and Rudy Gobert of the Utah Jazz

Young attends a charity event in 2019.

Young with his family in 2017, before he announced he would join the Sooners

Trae Young still considers himself a kid at heart. He is part of a close-knit family that loves spending time together. He has two sisters, Caitlyn and Camryn, and one brother, Timothy. Part of the reason Young attended Oklahoma was so his family would be

Young high-fives fans after a game with the Sooners.

just a short drive away. His off-season home is near his parents' home. That way, he can play basketball with his brother and show off his shots to his dad.

Young tries to connect with his fans. He is very active on social media. Young will answer questions from fans about basketball and other topics. He makes funny videos and sometimes watches his highlights from high school.

people who deal with mental health problems, and help prevent online bullying.

Young started the Trae Young Basketball Academy in Oklahoma. It teaches young athletes basketball skills and ways to become better people. He also partners with organizations in the Atlanta area, providing money to help families with medical bills.

"It's very important to me that I use my platform to make a difference and give back in any way I can," Young said.

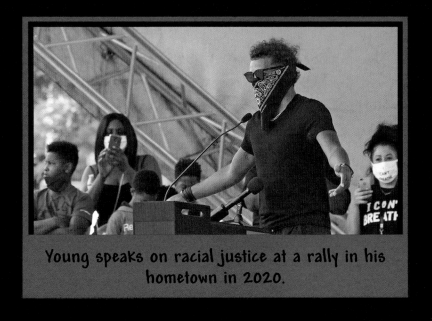

Young speaks on racial justice at a rally in his hometown in 2020.

Young got the nickname Ice Trae from Atlanta-based rapper Quavo, who worked on a song called "Ice Tray" in 2017.

Young recently signed a shoe deal with Adidas. His line of shoes includes high tops with bright colors and no laces. He played in special Ice Trae sneakers—which took their name from his nickname—during the NBA All-Star Game weekend. Icee, a famous frozen dessert, inspired the blue-and-red design on the shoes.

When the NBA paused the 2019–2020 season due to the COVID-19 pandemic, Young combined some of his favorite activities to keep up with fans. He took part in the NBA 2K20 video game challenge against other online players. Then he participated in the NBA HORSE competition, streaming shots from his court at home. In between trick shots, he gave out his phone number to everyone watching. "I've just been thinking of different ways to stay involved with my fans and with everybody in the basketball world," he said.

Young is introduced before a game in early 2020.

ALL-STAR RISING

Young dribbles the ball.

The NBA is the biggest challenge of Trae Young's basketball career. But he continues to prove he can handle just about anything.

Scoring a three-pointer in the NBA All-Star game made Young jump for joy.

In 2018, Young's first season with the Hawks got off to a great start. In his third game as a pro, he had 35 points and 11 assists. But the NBA season is long. It can wear down the most experienced players. Young struggled at times. He regained his form late in the year and finished strong. He vowed to play even better in his second season.

Young and his teammates celebrate his game-winning basket in March 2019.

Young improved his stats in nearly every category. Over 60 games, he averaged 29.6 points and 9.3 assists. Because of his popularity, fans voted him to start in the 2020 All-Star Game.

Young had a busy All-Star weekend in Chicago, Illinois. He participated in the Rising Stars game on Friday, scoring 18 points. He took part in the 3-Point Contest on Saturday, but he lost in the first round. Finally, on Sunday, he was among the NBA's biggest names as a member of Team Giannis in the All-Star Game. Young finished with a double-double: 10 points and 10 assists.

Even though Young has become an NBA superstar, he still wants more. The Hawks are rebuilding their team. Other talented new players have joined Atlanta. The next step is to get to the playoffs. One day, Young hopes to celebrate an NBA title. Some basketball reporters think he's good enough to be the league's most valuable player. Those goals are in reach for a player who most people thought was too small to make it.

"For me, being considered one of the best players in our league is an honor and a blessing," Young said. "But it's also motivation to keep going. I want to be even better."

In 2020, the Atlanta Hawks had gone 60 seasons without winning a championship, the second-longest drought in the NBA. Young hopes to change that for his team.

All-Star Stats

When Trae Young scored 50 points in a game, he joined an elite group of players to do so at such a young age. Here are the youngest players to score 50 or more points in a game:

Name	Points	Age
Brandon Jennings	55 points	20 years, 52 days
LeBron James	56 points	20 years, 80 days
Devin Booker	70 points	20 years, 145 days
LeBron James	52 points	20 years, 345 days
LeBron James	51 points	21 years, 22 days
Trae Young	50 points	21 years, 154 days

Glossary

arsenal: a collection of skills

double-double: when a player reaches double digits in two of the five main stats during a game. The five main stats are assists, blocked shots, points, rebounds, and steals.

drill: an exercise designed to improve a skill through repeated practice

floater: a one-handed midrange shot that flies slowly to the basket

free throw: an uncontested shot from behind the free throw line that is sometimes awarded when the other team commits a foul

jump shot: a shot made by jumping into the air and releasing the ball at the top of the jump

layup: a shot made from near the basket usually by bouncing the ball off the backboard

lob: a high arcing pass

point guard: the player in charge of a team's offense

prospect: someone who is very likely to be chosen for a job or position

7   Justin Benjamin, "Trae Young Had Miami Heat Matchup Circled on His Calendar in Order to Get Revenge," Heat Nation, May 7, 2020, https://heatnation.com/media/trae -young-had-heat-matchup-circled-his-calendar-order-get -revenge/.

12 Trae Young, in Adrian Wojnarowski, "Trae Young: Time Has Come for Me to Enter NBA Draft," ESPN, March 19, 2018, https://www.espn.com/nba/story/_/id/22838619/trae-young -come-enter-nba-draft.

16 Bryan Kalbrosky, "Trae Young May Already Have the Best Floating Jump Shot in the NBA," HoopsHype, March 19, 2019, https://hoopshype.com/2019/03/19/atlanta-hawks-trae-young -floater-teardrop-rookie-of-the-year/.

21 NBA, "Trae Young Receives January NBA Cares Community Assist Award Presented by Kaiser Permanente," press release, February 21, 2020, https://communityassist.nba.com /trae-young/.

23 Trae Young, in Kevin Pelton, "Young Shares His Phone Number with Fans," ESPN video, April 12, 2020, https://www .espn.com/nba/story/_/id/29021933/nba-horse-challenge -grading-every-player-quarterfinals.

27 Marc J. Spears, "How Trae Young Is Dealing with the Isolation of Social Distancing," Undefeated, March 25, 2020, https:// theundefeated.com/features/how-trae-young-is-dealing-with -isolation-of-social-distancing/.

Atlanta Hawks
https://www.nba.com/hawks/

Geoffreys, Clayton. *Trae Young: The Inspiring Story of One of Basketball's Star Guards*. Winter Park, FL: Calvintir Books, 2020.

Levit, Joe. *Basketball's G.O.A.T.: Michael Jordan, LeBron James, and More*. Minneapolis: Lerner Publications, 2020.

Lynne, Douglas. *Trae Young: NBA Star*. Mendota Heights, MN: North Star Editions, 2020.

Trae Young
https://www.nba.com/players/trae/young/1629027

Trae Young
https://www.traeyoung11.net

Index

Photo Acknowledgments

Image credits: Todd Kirkland/Getty Images, pp. 4-5, 6, 24; AP Photo/Brian Rothmuller, pp. 8, 16; AP Photo/John Bazemore, p. 9; AP Photo/Matthew Visinsky, p. 11; AP Photo/Robert Backman, p. 12; AP Photo/Uncredited, p. 13; AP Photo/Sue Ogrocki, pp. 15, 20, 21; AP Photo/David Banks, pp. 17, 25; lev radin/Shutterstock.com, p. 18; AP Photo/Steve Sisney, p. 19; AP Photo/John Amis, pp. 23, 26.

Cover: Todd Kirkland/Getty Images.